The *Shakespeare Library*

Shakespeare's Players

WENDY GREENHILL

HEAD OF EDUCATION
ROYAL SHAKESPEARE COMPANY

and

First published in Great Britain by Heinemann Library
Halley Court, Jordan Hill, Oxford OX2 8EJ
a division of Reed Educational & Professional Publishing Ltd

OXFORD FLORENCE PRAGUE MADRID ATHENS
MELBOURNE AUCKLAND KUALA LUMPUR SINGAPORE TOKYO
IBADAN NAIROBI KAMPALA JOHANNESBURG GABORONE
PORTSMOUTH NH (USA) CHICAGO MEXICO CITY SAO PAULO

Designed by Ken Vail Graphic Design, Cambridge
Printed in the U.K. by Jarrold Book Printing Ltd, Thetford

00 99 98 97 96
10 9 8 7 6 5 4 3 2 1

British Library Cataloguing in Publication Data
Greenhill, Wendy
Shakespeare's Players. – (The Shakespeare Library)
1. Shakespeare, William, 1546–1616 – Juvenile literature
2. English Drama – Early modern and Elizabethan, 1500–1600 – Juvenile literature
I. Title II. Wignall, Paul
822.3'3

ISBN 0 431 07526 3

Acknowledgements
The authors and publishers would like to thank the following for permission to reproduce photographs and other illustrative material:

The Bodleian Library, pages 6, 17, 23;
The Bridgeman Art Library, pages 19, 26, 27, 29;
The British Library, page 8;
The British Museum, pages 11, 18;
The Trustees of Dulwich Picture Library, page 28;
The Guildhall Library, page 9;
Knowsley Hall, Lancs, page 7;
The Master and Fellows of Magdalene College, Cambridge, page 21;
The Mansell Collection, page 15;
The National Portrait Gallery, page 14;
The National Trust, page 10;
The Shakespeare Centre Library, Stratford-Upon-Avon, pages 16, 30;
Simon Wingfield Digby, Sherbourne Castle Estates, page 5;
University of Utrecht Library, page 13.

Cover photograph reproduced with permission of
the Master and Fellows of Magdalene College, Cambridge.

Our thanks to Jean Black and Andrew Gurr for their comments in the preparation of this book.

Every effort has been made to contact copyright holders of any material reproduced in this book. Any omissions will be rectified in subsequent printings if notice is given to the Publisher.

In preparing this book, the authors have used *William Shakespeare The Complete Works*, Clarendon Press, Oxford 1986.

CONTENTS

SPECTACLES AND SHOWS

illiam Shakespeare was born in 1564 and grew up during the reign of Queen Elizabeth I (1558–1603). It was a time of great change in many areas of life.

Elizabeth put a lot of energy into making her country peaceful and prosperous. After years of struggle, English religion was finally established as Protestant. Although there were still many Roman Catholics, they had to worship in secret and were looked at with suspicion – and might be executed as traitors.

English explorers such as Drake and Raleigh were among the first to reach the Americas and to sail round the world. The House of Commons became more important as a place where Members of Parliament from all over the country could express their views to the Queen and her ministers. Many new schools were opened and there was enthusiasm for learning and scientific discovery. The printing and selling of books flourished in London. At the same time, the kinds of entertainment which had been part of life for generations took a great leap forward and a professional theatre developed rapidly in London. Players (actors) began to enjoy fame and fortune as a reward for their talent and hard work.

POPULAR ENTERTAINMENT

The Elizabethans liked to enjoy themselves. Stratford-on-Avon, Shakespeare's home town, had fairs twice a year, in May and in September, and in his plays Shakespeare often refers to popular entertainments he would have enjoyed there: wrestling, bear-baiting, music, dancing, fast-talking salesmen with bargains to sell, stunts and spectacular sights. Much of this is still part of the fun of fairs and carnivals today.

THE QUEEN'S PROGRESSES

Queen Elizabeth toured the country regularly. These royal tours were called 'progresses'. She stayed at the great houses of noblemen and made sure that she was seen in all her glory by as many of her subjects as possible, arriving in a very grand procession. Elizabethans from the Queen down loved a good show and her hosts went to elaborate lengths to organise spectacular entertainment to welcome her and keep her happy. Fireworks, pageants, mock battles and dramatic scenes, music and displays of dancing greeted the Queen and the crowds who had turned out to see her. Perhaps Shakespeare saw the entertainments arranged for her when she visited the Earl of Leicester at Kenilworth, just a few miles from Stratford, in 1575.

THE MYSTERY CYCLES

In the centuries before Elizabeth reigned, another form of dramatic entertainment had been developed by the church in which parts of the Bible were acted out. The craftsmen's guilds (also known as 'mysteries') took over this activity and performed plays tracing the story of God's creation of the world, through the birth and crucifixion of Jesus and on to the end of the world. Although the subject of these 'mystery' plays was serious, their style was sometimes earthy and comic. There is a play telling the story of Noah's Ark, for instance, in which Mrs Noah is a lively comic character, always nagging and scolding her husband.

The tradition of putting on religious plays began to die out after England became a Protestant country during the reign of Henry VIII, and the last performance of a complete cycle was at Coventry in 1580. It is possible that the sixteen-year-old Shakespeare would have seen it.

Queen Elizabeth I liked to travel around in great style. Here she is, aged 67, in procession, surrounded by her courtiers.

'ROGUES AND VAGABONDS'

By the time of Elizabeth, non-religious plays were very popular too. As a boy, Shakespeare would have seen performances by groups of travelling players who visited Stratford. The players' companies had a variety of plays they could put on. No doubt comedies were the most popular, but they also performed plays about important moments in English history, and morality plays in which good triumphed (eventually) over evil or where temptation was resisted.

Some of them were written by well-educated university men but most were knocked together by the actors themselves based on their own reading, on current events, or on adaptations of popular stories.

Town councils paid the players and helped organise their visits, but Elizabethan citizens were never sure that they were respectable. There was great fear of vagrants, poor people who wandered around the countryside homeless and hungry. They were suspected of violent crime, robbery and of spreading disease. Harsh laws were passed which aimed at preventing vagrancy. The poor were supposed to stay in their home parish where they might get help; people with no home and no money were punished and sent packing. Any travelling player or entertainer who was not part of a nobleman's household was classed as one of these 'rogues and vagabonds' and liable to be punished. So groups of players had to gain the favour of a rich man, and be adopted as his servants. This gave them an official home even though they still spent time touring the country.

A woodcut from the title page of John Taylor's *The Praise, Antiquity and Commodity of Beggary, Beggars and Begging.*

THE EARL OF LEICESTER'S MEN

In 1572, the law against vagabonds was revised and made stricter. Punishments could vary from whipping and branding to death. Companies of players had to take even greater care to be under the protection of noblemen.

One of the earliest successful companies was the Earl of Leicester's Men, which included a carpenter turned actor, James Burbage. A letter from Burbage to Leicester shows how sponsorship of the arts by the rich and powerful has always been a part of English theatre. Burbage was, however, careful to say that in this case it wouldn't cost the Earl of Leicester any money at all!

'We therefore your humble servants ... your players ... are bold to trouble your Lordship with this our suit [request], humbly desiring your honour (as you have always been our good Lord and Master) you will now vouchsafe [be willing] to retain [keep] us at this present as your household servants ... not that we mean to crave any further stipend [salary] and benefit at your Lordship's hands but our liveries [special clothing] as we have had, and also your honour's licence [permission] to certify that we are your household servants when we shall have occasion to travel amongst our friends as we do usually once a year, and as other noblemen's players do ...'

Two years later the Earl of Leicester's Men did even better for themselves. On 10 May 1574, the Queen gave them her own protection, not only to perform throughout the country but also, and most valuably:

'... within our City of London and liberties of the same.'

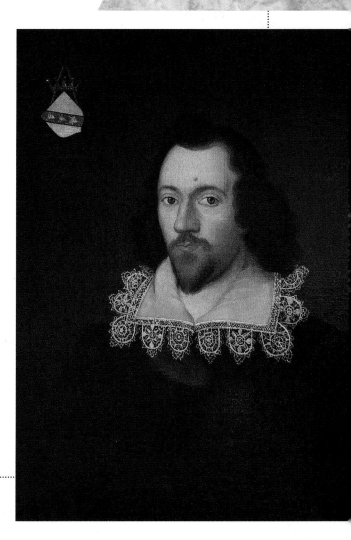

A portrait of Ferdinando Stanley, Lord Strange. Many of the company under his protection were founder-sharers of the Lord Chamberlain's Men in 1594.

PLAYING IN LONDON

In the 1560s and 1570s, companies of players toured the cities and market towns of England. They were also invited to perform for the Queen and her court at the royal palaces. London was the great magnet, drawing people to it as it does today. It was the centre of thriving activity, and the players wanted to be a more permanent part of it. Two men, James Burbage and his brother-in-law, John Brayne, provided the first theatre buildings which gave them a base in London.

THE RED LION

Brayne started with the conversion of a farmhouse, the Red Lion, into a playhouse, but it is not known if this was ever finished. We have some details about this building, showing that it included several features which were also found in the inns and innyards where plays had been performed in the past. Galleries of seating enclosed a courtyard in which a stage was placed. The stage had a trap door and was raised on barrels with a space under it. At the back was a kind of tower. This set up three 'levels', meant to be of heaven, earth and hell.

Even if it was never used for performances, the Red Lion design formed the basis for all the later playhouses.

THE THEATRE

From 1576 Burbage and Brayne worked together on the building of the first playhouse we can be sure was used. It was called the Theatre. They raised nearly £700 (equivalent to seven years' income of a rich merchant), leased a plot of land in Shoreditch, and quickly got on with the building.

An indoor playhouse (probably the Cockpit) during a performance in 1632.

Soon after, a rival playhouse, the Curtain, opened nearby. Both the Theatre and the Curtain were used by various companies and proved a great success. Clergymen began to complain that 'a filthy play' could attract a full audience to these playhouses even on 'The Lord's Day' (Sunday).

Why were the players so successful? Animal fights drew big crowds and remained popular, but plays appealed because they included something for everyone. The performances mixed comedy with tragedy, high emotion with knockabout fun, poetry, music, swordfights and philosophical reflection. Audiences went to 'hear a play'. Elizabethans loved the spoken word and the cut and thrust of argument and debate, and the theatre mirrored this. They were used to using their imagination so they could share the on-stage action in their hearts and minds.

AUDIENCE INVOLVEMENT

They didn't listen in silence. Public performances took place in the open air during the afternoon, and this gives us an important clue. You went to a play in the 1590s as you might go to a football match, a funfair, or a rock concert today. There was noise, heckling, eating and drinking. The audience shared everything with the characters – laughing, crying, groaning, applauding. Packed in tight, often standing up, they were close enough to the stage to get totally involved.

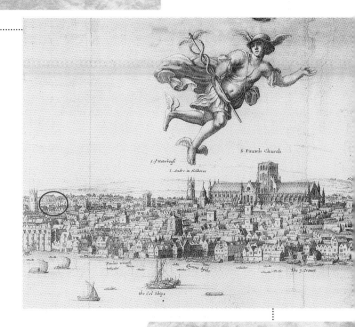

A section of Hollar's 'Long View' of London, 1644. The circled building is probably the Blackfriars Theatre where the King's Men played.

There was a lot of bad behaviour. Henry Chettle wrote in 1592 that 'the young people of the city' should either

> *'... abstain [keep away] altogether from plays or ... use [behave] themselves after a more quiet order [way].'*

Some companies, including Shakespeare's, tried to encourage a more respectable audience. The playhouses north of the river – the Curtain and the Red Bull, for instance – continued to be seen as rowdy and often indecent. The new theatres on the Bankside, such as the Globe and the Swan, distanced themselves from this older, often crude, type of performance and attracted a more upmarket audience.

PLAYING IN THE COUNTRY

In the days of Queen Elizabeth and King James, actors generally preferred to be in London. London was where the best work could be found. London was where you were 'noticed'. London was where you had the best chance of earning a good living. It's not much different today: actors like to be in London; it's the centre of their profession. But actors have to go where the work is, and the managers of theatre companies like to take their productions to be seen by as many people as possible; the bigger the audience, the greater the income.

Charlecote Park, near Stratford, where Queen Elizabeth stayed in 1566.

ON TOUR

All the early acting companies spent time in London but they also went out on tour. There were a number of reasons for this. First of all players had always been 'travelling players', setting up their stage wherever they could get the work: in the houses of the nobility, in the market halls of towns, at fairs, in the courtyards of inns. Most players who worked at the Theatre, the Curtain, the Rose and the Globe had started out 'on the road'.

Another reason was that players might accompany the Queen on her progresses through the country, where she showed herself to her people. They were available to entertain the Queen, but were no doubt happy to pick up extra work on the way. They might also accompany noblemen to their home areas – the Earl of Leicester's Men were often in Warwickshire. Or they might go further afield – again, the Earl of Leicester's Men went with their patron into the Low Countries where he was fighting a war against Spain.

A simple stage in 1600.

Another reason for touring was that even acting companies with a London home could find the theatres closed because of plague or fear of rebellion. If they could get a licence from the Lord Chamberlain, they would be able to tour, and not lose too much income.

VISITING STRATFORD

Companies of actors regularly visited Stratford during Shakespeare's boyhood. His father was a man of status in the town and his family would have had good seats for the performances in the Guild Hall. When he was 23, the Queen's Men came to town. That year, 1587, they also toured to Bath, Leicester, York, Coventry (twice), Aldeburgh in Suffolk (three times), and probably elsewhere. Stratford Corporation paid the company twenty shillings – a large sum in those days.

When they visited Stratford, the Queen's Men were probably one player short because on 13 June 1587 William Knell, one of their leading players, was killed in a duel at Thame in Oxfordshire. Did Shakespeare replace him? We have no proof, of course, but it is not impossible. However, we know that soon after he was in London, and beginning to make a name for himself.

In London, Shakespeare was with a company that came to be called the Chamberlain's Men. They often went on tour, but we don't know if Shakespeare went with them: he may have gone back to Stratford to look after his business there, and maybe to write. In 1594 they were in Marlborough, Wiltshire, where the mayor gave them two shillings and eight pence. They were back in 1597, when they were given six shillings and fourpence. Renamed the King's Men, they returned in 1606 for twenty three shillings and fourpence, and again in 1608 for twenty shillings. All of this was in addition to the takings from the performances themselves.

STYLES OF ACTING

Today we are used to several different styles of acting. In television soap operas and in films we expect actors to be very natural and 'true to life'. If we go to see a musical we accept a larger than life style of acting and elaborate stage design; the exaggeration has its own energy and impact which we enjoy. It is disastrous if actors confuse the two styles: we would laugh at 'over-the-top' emotion in a soap opera on television; and we would be bored by too much realism in a stage musical. Getting the style right for the type of play and place where it is performed is the essence of good acting. The Elizabethans were as critical of their players as we are today, and there are many accounts which analyse styles of performance and give advice.

We know that the players in the big public playhouses like the Globe acted on a stage thrust out into the audience which surrounded it on all four sides. Acting in the middle of 3000 noisy people in broad daylight must have demanded very confident performances, played to catch the eye and ear of everyone around. It must have been a larger than life style. As women's parts were played by boys and men, it is obvious that Elizabethan acting was a long way from modern realism.

THE LANGUAGE

We also know what the players said. The language of Elizabethan theatre did not simply copy the language of the street. Most plays contain 'blank verse': dramatic poetry with a strong and subtle rhythm in a particular pattern – the iambic pentameter.

Repetition, the balance of the lines, images – word pictures – are all used to convey complicated thoughts and feelings. When Shakespeare's Romeo realises that it is morning and he has to leave Juliet, perhaps never to see her again, he describes the dawn poetically:

**'Night's candles are burnt out, and jocund day
Stands tip-toe on the misty mountain tops.'**

He follows this with an absolutely direct statement:

'I must be gone and live, or stay and die.'

Both types of language tell us how he feels, but the player has to switch from delicate pictures of dawn to brutal realism in a way which is not usual in everyday speech. He has to express the full meaning and feeling in his tone of voice and use of pauses and emphasis. He has to use the poetry and not be embarrassed by it.

MOVEMENT AND GESTURE

Elizabethans expected players to match their movements and gestures to the meaning of the words. But they disliked performances where the actors' gestures seemed artificial or untruthful. As a character in John Marston's play, *Antonio's Revenge*, says:

'... would'st have me turn rank mad,
Or ring my face with mimic action,
Stamp, curse, weepe, rage, and
then thy bosom strike?
Away, 'tis apeish action,
player-like. '

A drawing of the interior of the Swan Theatre by Johannes de Witt. See how the stage is surrounded by galleries where the audience would sit.

THE MASTER
OF THE REVELS

Elizabethan England had many enemies. As a Protestant country it was under attack from Catholic France and Spain. Elizabeth and her ministers spent much time and effort trying to secure their country from foreign invasion. But they were also worried about enemies at home. There were Catholic sympathisers, of course, but there were also many other discontented people, ranging from offended or ambitious nobles to the poor victims of economic and social change.

Ben Jonson – actor and playwright. His plays were performed by the Chamberlain's Men and his masques entertained King James.

By the 1580s, London had become the focus for England's energy and for its troubles too. The rise of the new popular entertainment in the playhouses had its dangers. Plays not only entertained, they also communicated information, gave opinions and whipped up emotions. The Queen and her ministers in the Privy Council knew that controlling the players was an important way of avoiding rebellion.

THE LORD CHAMBERLAIN

The official responsible for this was the Lord Chamberlain, who took charge of all court entertainments. From 1585–96 the Lord Chamberlain was Henry, Lord Hunsdon. When Shakespeare and his colleagues were successful in getting his protection in 1594, and were able to call themselves the Chamberlain's Men, they knew they had reached the top of their profession. Other companies were still selected to play at court, but the Chamberlain's Men were most often preferred. This gave them money, status and security in a generally insecure world. In 1603, when the Queen died, they were renamed the King's Men and became a part of King James's own household.

The officials who managed the day-to-day business of the Lord Chamberlain worked in the Revels Office in St John's Gate. The people who worked there were the Master of the Revels, a couple of clerks, and the Yeoman of the Revels. The Yeoman was essentially responsible for the care and maintenance of the huge wardrobe of clothes (often cast-offs from noblemen and women), but he also helped with the staging of court entertainments. At first he was a tailor; by King James's day he was more a professional man of the theatre.

SIR EDMUND TILNEY

The Master of the Revels had a much bigger job. From 1581, the Master was Sir Edmund Tilney. His first task was to find the best players and companies to perform at court, not only at the regular times of feasting such as Christmas, but also for special events such as visits by foreign ambassadors or royalty. One way of managing this was to create a company made up of the best twelve actors in England. Formed in 1583, the Queen's Men, as it was called, survived for nearly ten years before competition caught up with it. But Tilney also regularly auditioned companies, choosing plays that had been successful in the public theatres to be presented again at court.

Tilney's second main function was to control the companies, plays and, from the 1590s, the playhouses themselves. He had to read every new play and could demand changes or even refuse to allow its performance if he thought it contained material likely to offend the Queen or disturb the peace. It cost 7 shillings to have a licence from Sir Edmund, when admission to a play was twopence. In 1607, Tilney began to license plays for printing, making a charge of twenty shillings.

A page from the Master of the Revels' account book for 1604-5, including *Henry V* and *The Merchant of Venice* (twice) by 'Shaxberd' (Shakespeare).

THE LORD CHAMBERLAIN'S MEN

SHARERS

The companies were always teams of actors, but from time to time – say if their patron died – they would break up and reform. For this reason we often find the same group of names in different companies over the years. Companies were made up of two sorts of actors: sharers, who took a share in the risks as well as the profits; and hired men, who were taken on for short periods of time. In 1594 one group formed themselves into a new company, the Lord Chamberlain's Men, under the protection of the Lord Chamberlain.

A portrait, said to be of William Shakespeare, by Gerard Soest.

By 1596 there were eight sharers in the company: Richard Burbage (the son of James), Will Kemp, Thomas Pope, George Bryan (soon to be replaced by Henry Condell), Augustine Phillips, William Sly, John Heminges – and William Shakespeare. They acted in the first performances of many of Shakespeare's plays at the Theatre: *A Midsummer Night's Dream*, *As You Like It* and *The Merchant of Venice*, for instance.

A NEW BUSINESS DEAL

When they moved across the river to the Globe in 1599, Kemp left them, but was replaced by Robert Armin. At the Globe a new arrangement was made and Shakespeare, Pope, Phillips, Heminges and (briefly) Kemp were sharers in the theatre's profits as well as in the company. The sharers quickly became rich men. In 1603, Queen Elizabeth died and the new King, James I, gave the Lord Chamberlain's Men his own patronage. The King's Men, as they now became, eventually took on a second, indoor, theatre at the Blackfriars, giving the sharers still greater wealth. It was for this company that Shakespeare wrote some of his greatest plays, including *Othello*, *King Lear*, *Macbeth* and *The Tempest*.

JOHN HEMINGES

By 1611 John Heminges, who had been an actor for over twenty years, with the Queen's Men, Lord Strange's Men and then the Lord Chamberlain's Men, had effectively become the King's Men's business manager. He received the payment for their performances, which he would then share out around his colleagues. They trusted him, and he took his responsibilities seriously.

Heminges married in 1588. His wife, Rebecca, was the widow of the actor William Knell who was killed in a duel at Thame in Oxfordshire in 1587. They lived near the Globe in Southwark, and had fourteen children, some of whom died young. In 1611, when Heminges's daughter, Thomasina, was sixteen, she married one of the King's Men, William Ostler. Unfortunately Ostler died in 1614 without making a will and Thomasina had to make special arrangements about his shares in the Globe and Blackfriars theatres, asking her father to hold them in trust for her.

Before long Thomasina, still only 20, got involved in a love affair with Walt Raleigh, the son of the explorer, and caused a scandal. Walt was quite a rogue who must have insulted Thomasina publicly because she took him to court and was awarded damages of £250 – a huge sum compared to what a student might have lived off for a whole year – £20! But John Heminges clearly didn't trust

Thomasina with the fortune that was growing from her late husband's shares. She had to take her father to court twice, demanding payments of £700 which she said he owed her. Both times they settled out of court and the story fades away. However, the sums of money involved were enormous and clearly show the wealth that a successful actor or theatre shareholder could expect to make in a very short time.

Some Elizabethan characters – including Falstaff on the left – from *The Wits*, 1662.

THE BOY PLAYERS

One of the most distinctive, and to our eyes unusual, features of the playing companies was that they were made up of men and boys. Women did not perform in the professional English theatre until the 1660s. Boys joined the companies as apprentices to the senior actors. In this way they learnt their craft. Some actors continued to specialise in female roles when they had grown up, and certainly some of the characters created by Shakespeare – Lady Macbeth and Queen Cleopatra, for instance – needed exceptional skill and talent to bring them off.

There were also acting companies made up of only boys. Some grew out of London choir-schools but others were quite definitely professional ventures run by businessmen with the aim of making money.

ACTING AT SCHOOL

Throughout the sixteenth century it was quite usual for schoolmasters to encourage their pupils to act out scenes and dialogues. This was seen as a way of teaching them how to use the English language well, even to replace Latin as the language of learning. Shakespeare was taught in this way in Stratford, at the King's New School. These performances were very respectable, rather like today's school play, and often included sophisticated singing, especially if the school was linked to a cathedral choir. The plays might be written by the schoolmasters themselves, often translating or adapting old Latin plays. A good example is the comedy *Ralph Roister Doister*, written by Nicholas Udal, a headmaster of Eton in the 1550s. This combines the techniques of the Latin plays with racy English humour, and it became very popular.

Choristers –
Children of the
Chapel Royal.

COMMERCIAL THEATRE COMPANIES

The first company of boy actors created to run a business were the Chapel Children, who performed at the Blackfriars on the north bank of the Thames from 1576. This company was closed down in 1590 but revived as a business venture in 1599. These companies reached the peak of their popularity between about 1600 and 1608, when plays were specially written for them by professional playwrights such as Ben Jonson and John Marston. They included the 'Paul's Boys' and the 'Revels Children'.

The Chapel Children (or 'Blackfriars Boys') were managed after 1599 by Henry Evans. As well as encouraging his boys to behave in an arrogant way (Shakespeare in *Hamlet* refers to them as 'little eyases' – eagles), he had a strong sense of his own importance. He was so keen to build up his company that in December 1600 he kidnapped a boy, Thomas Clifton, on his way home from school. His father complained but Evans told him that he had official permission to take any boy he liked into the company. Mr Clifton went further and complained to the Privy Council, the Queen's closest advisers. It worked: Thomas Clifton was released within twenty-four hours.

For a while the boy companies were very popular, though many attempts were made to shut them down. Shakespeare never wrote for them – indeed for a few years they were 'the opposition' but one or two of their plays were of lasting importance, and a few boy actors joined the adult companies when they grew up. Nathan Field was one of the Chapel Children until 1610, in spite of the fact that his father was a clergyman who preached regularly against plays. Field joined the King's Men in 1616, probably taking over Shakespeare's share when he died. He went on to become one of the leading actors in the company.

The famous boy player Nathan Field, who replaced Shakespeare as a sharer in the King's Men in 1616.

RICHARD TARLTON

There are some performers and entertainers whose appeal is very wide. Some years ago Eric Morecambe and Ernie Wise had a way of making the whole country laugh, and their television Christmas shows are still repeated regularly. Along with Frankie Howerd, Tony Hancock and Spike Milligan, they not only caught the mood of Britain in the 1950s and 1960s, but also influenced many other comedians and writers who followed them, such as Paul Merton, Victoria Wood, and Vic Reeves and Bob Mortimer.

A GREAT ENTERTAINER

In the 1570s the first great English clown came on the scene. His name was Richard Tarlton. He, too, was amazingly popular: he acted in stage plays in London and on tour, he entertained Queen Elizabeth and her court at banquets, and he seems even to have had a career as one of the first 'stand-up comedians', performing in taverns and inns in London. Like all the great entertainers, there are many stories about Tarlton's life and his humour. They were collected in a book called *Tarlton's Jests* printed in 1600, more than ten years after his death. Many are no doubt true, but some are just 'good stories' which got linked to him as the funniest man of his day.

Like many comedians, what Tarlton did and said in public probably hid his real self very successfully. For instance, he liked to present himself as a poor man, but we know that when he died his mother claimed that she'd been done out of £700 in his will: a small fortune in those days. Pictures show him dressed as a peasant, but when he died he had official positions at court. His wit was sharp, and he was also a master fencer – a gentleman's sport.

One of Tarlton's comic advantages was his appearance. He was short, with a flat nose and a squint. He was good at playing the stupid countryman. It's said that one of his favourite tricks was sticking his head through the stage curtains during serious scenes: the sight of his face was enough to bring the house down. No one knew what was going to happen next when he was on stage.

Tarlton also had a tremendous skill as an improviser, especially responding to rowdiness and heckling from the audience, just like stand-up comedians today. In fact his stage roles often invited insults – he listened to them, then quickly turned them round against those attacking him, and humiliated them in turn.

THE QUEEN'S MEN

As an actor he worked with the Queen's Men, who appeared at court, but also toured the country. He also worked alone and was often invited to banquets where his combination of wit and insult, and his performance as a countryman trying to be fashionable, was very popular. Queen Elizabeth loved him, and he once made her helpless with laughter by engaging in a mock duel with her favourite little dog. When not on stage or at court he seems to have performed in taverns – which he may have owned – in Gracechurch Street in London. Wherever he played he was a great – and dangerous – improviser.

Tarlton died in 1588 and was buried on 3 September at St Leonard's, Shoreditch. But he was not forgotten. Shakespeare must have known his work – he may even have written the part of Launce in *The Two Gentlemen of Verona* for Tarlton and his dog. And he also remembered him when he was writing *Hamlet* – the dead jester Yorick is almost certainly a tribute to Tarlton.

Richard Tarlton, with pipe and drum, dressed as a countryman.

WILLIAM KEMP

The next great clown after Richard Tarlton was William Kemp. The whole of Kemp's career is linked with the acting companies, and yet he seems to have kept himself separate from them. In 1580 he was one of the Earl of Leicester's Men. By 1585 he was with the Earl in the Low Countries (Holland and Belgium), but as in records his name is kept separate from the other players, he may have had a special role, almost like that of a court jester.

That year, 1585, Sir Philip Sidney, Leicester's nephew, gave Kemp a letter to deliver to his wife. But unfortunately Kemp gave it to the wrong person, causing much embarrassment. A few years later, Kemp was another inefficient postman when he played Peter in *Romeo and Juliet*!

In 1586 Richard Kemp was one of five English actors performing at Elsinore Castle in Denmark (the setting for Shakespeare's play *Hamlet* written just a few years later). In 1588 the Earl of Leicester died and Kemp joined another acting company, called Lord Strange's Men.

WITH THE LORD CHAMBERLAIN'S MEN

A number of actors, including Kemp, left Lord Strange's Men in 1594 to join the Lord Chamberlain's Men, the company with which Shakespeare was to earn his fortune. Kemp probably played Bottom in *A Midsummer Night's Dream*, Launcelot Gobbo in *The Merchant of Venice*, Costard in *Love's Labour's Lost*, Dogberry in *Much Ado About Nothing*, and Peter in *Romeo and Juliet*. It is also likely that he played Falstaff in *Henry IV parts 1 and 2* and *The Merry Wives of Windsor*.

Where Richard Tarlton had been a great improviser, Kemp's talent was his energetic physical presence. He was a good dancer, which must have been shown to great advantage in the Bergamasque, or dance, that ends *A Midsummer Night's Dream*. This is the dance which the 'actors' in the play of *Pyramus and Thisbe* put on to try to get back into favour with their audience after their terrible performance. In Kemp's day most plays ended with some kind of dance to send the audience home happy. These dances jigs were generally bawdy and suggestive; and very popular!

MARATHON DANCES

Kemp decided to cash in on the popularity of his jigs. In 1599 he had become a sharer in the new Globe theatre. If he had stayed there he would have become a rich man, like Shakespeare and the other shareholders, but Kemp fell out with members of the company and left the same year. It was then he decided to dance from London to Norwich. It was a fantastic feat of skill and stamina. He completed the journey in nine days (with rests in between), and still had the energy to jump over a churchyard wall when he got to Norwich! He wrote a book about it called *Nine Daies Wonder*. In it he also attacks the players at the Globe – calling them 'Shakerags', an obvious reference to Shakespeare. The jig to Norwich was so successful that in 1601 he danced right across Europe to Rome.

By September 1601 he was back in England. He then led a company of actors into Germany but by Christmas of that year he had returned to England again, working with the Earl of Worcester's Men, who copied some of the more successful ideas of the Chamberlain's Men. But Kemp could never settle. He liked to do his own thing, which meant jigs. His popularity didn't lead to wealth, however. In 1602 he borrowed twenty shillings from a playhouse owner, Phillip Henslowe. William Kemp died, probably of the plague, in 1603.

The frontispiece of William Kemp's book, *Nine Daies Wonder*, his own account of his jig from London to Norwich in 1600.

Kemps nine daies vvonder.

Performed in a daunce from London to Norwich.

Containing the pleasure, paines and kinde entertainment of William Kemp betweene London and that Citty in his late Morrice.

Wherein is somewhat set downe worth note; to reprooue the flaunders spred of him: many things merry, nothing hurtfull.

Written by himselfe to satisfie his friends.

LONDON

Printed by E. A. for Nicholas Ling, and are to be solde at his shop at the west doore of Saint Paules Church. 1600.

ROBERT ARMIN

All the acting companies needed a specialist clown, with his own particular skills. When William Kemp jigged out of the Lord Chamberlain's Men in 1599, he had to be replaced. There is no obvious clown's role in Shakespeare's *Julius Caesar*, performed in the autumn of 1599 (although *Julius Caesar* would have been followed by a jig, in the usual way). And he is not mentioned in the list of players for Ben Jonson's comedy, *Every Man in His Humour*, performed by the company at the same time. Eventually, however, Kemp's successor was found. And in Robert Armin they found a talented performer who inspired Shakespeare into creating some of his greatest comic characters.

Armin was born at King's Lynn in Norfolk, the son of a tailor. He was well educated, speaking both Latin and Italian, and came to London to be apprenticed to a goldsmith (learning the trade) who lived in Lombard Street. In London he got to know Richard Tarlton.

A tribute to Tarlton published in 1600, called *Tarlton's Jests*, includes a section called 'How Tarlton made Armin his adopted sonne, to succeed him'. It tells how Tarlton and Armin used to exchange witty poems while Armin was still an apprentice. Tarlton's verse ended with the lines:

**'My adopted sonne therefore be
To enjoy my clown's suit after me.'**

The story then describes how Armin started going to watch Tarlton perform. In a sense he became an apprentice clown, learning a new trade.

When *Tarlton's Jests* was printed in August 1600, Robert Armin was a well-known member of the Chamberlain's Men.

'... and at this houre performes the same, where, at the Globe on the Banks side men may see him.'

THE WRITER

Like all clowns, Armin brought his own skills and personality to his work. He was an exceptionally good mime and mimic. He must have had a fine singing voice because many of the roles Shakespeare created for him include songs – above all, Feste in *Twelfth Night* and Autolycus in *The Winter's Tale*. He also had a sharp wit and was well read. As a young man he wrote ballads – songs telling a story – and in about 1598 wrote a play called *The Two Maids of More-clacke*, which was printed in 1609.

His clowning was not the improvising knockabout of Tarlton or Kemp; it was funny, but often very sad as well. In *The Two Maids of More-clacke* he probably played the part of 'John of the Hospital', a 'natural fool' or 'simpleton' who is described as having:

**'A nurse to tend him, put on his clothes
Yet was a man of old years when he died.'**

It was Armin who played the Fool in *King Lear* as well as the bitter Thersites in *Troilus and Cressida*, and Ariel or Caliban in *The Tempest*.

The title page of Robert Armin's *The History of the Two Maids of More-clacke*. The figure is almost certainly Armin in the character of 'John of the Hospital'.

THE
History of the two Maids of More-clacke,

VVith the life and simple maner of IOHN
in the Hospitall.

Played by the Children of the Kings
Maiesties Reuels.

VVritten by ROBERT ARMIN, seruant to the Kings
most excellent Maiestie.

LONDON,
Printed by *N.O.* for *Thomas Archer,* and is to be sold at his
shop in Popes-head Pallace, 1 6 0 9.

RICHARD BURBAGE

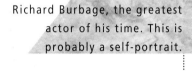

Richard Burbage was probably born in 1567 and began acting as a boy player at the Theatre, managed by his father. The Burbages were strong characters. James was often involved in disputes with visiting companies over money, and Richard was happy to join in. There is even a story that he threatened his aunt's servants with a broom handle when she came to argue with James about money owed to her. Richard and Cuthbert were involved in the dismantling of the Theatre when the lease was up in 1599, and the building of the new Globe from its timbers. Richard was evidently a tough man of action like his father.

A LEADING COMPANY MEMBER

Richard was also one of the leading sharers in the Chamberlain's Men from 1594. He took a major part in looking after its affairs, both practical and artistic, right up to his death in 1619, three years after Shakespeare's. The company's rise to fame and fortune and its long term success must be due to a great extent to Richard Burbage's skills as a leading actor.

James Burbage not only kick-started the professional theatre in England by building the Theatre, he also produced two sons who followed in his footsteps. Cuthbert worked in the management of playhouses and Richard became the greatest actor of his time and the first to play most of Shakespeare's major characters.

THE STAR

For over twenty years Shakespeare wrote his plays with Burbage clearly in mind. They must have discussed and tried out ideas together just as writers and actors do today. The suffering of King Lear and Othello, the intelligence of Hamlet, the devilish wit of Richard III, all suggest that Burbage was an immensely powerful and versatile actor. These qualities are mentioned by writers of the time, all of whom praise his ability to transform himself with the character and to suit his actions to the meaning of the words.

Shakespeare gives Hamlet a speech in which he advises a group of players about acting. Since this was spoken by Burbage we can take it to be a statement of what he and Shakespeare were trying to achieve on stage. Hamlet warns against over-acting, attacking players who:

'... tear a passion to tatters, to very rags, to split the ears
of the groundlings ... I would have such a fellow whipped ...'

And he says that the purpose of acting is to show a truthful picture of life to the audience:

'... to hold as 'twere the mirror up to nature.'

The Globe Theatre: Burbage performed some of the greatest roles in the theatre here for twenty years.

A GREAT LOSS

Burbage died at the age of 52, the same age as William Shakespeare, and three years later than him. To his contemporaries it seemed like the end of an era:

'He's gone, and with him what a world are dead.
No more young Hamlet, old Hieronymo,
King Lear, the grieved Moor, and more beside
That liv'd in him, have now for ever died.'

Or, as an anonymous admirer wrote, simply:

Exit Burbage

THE OPPOSITION

Although Shakespeare, the Burbage family and their company dominated the London theatre, they didn't have it all their own way. There was another powerful and successful partnership between the theatre manager and businessman Phillip Henslowe and the actor Edward Alleyn. They both became rich men, showing once again that, for the Elizabethans, art and business could make a good partnership.

THE ROSE PLAYHOUSE

Like James Burbage, Henslowe started life as an apprentice learning a trade, but he didn't abandon it to be an actor. He cleverly married his master's widow and became a rich man overnight. He always had several business interests on the go but his main project was the theatre. In 1587 he built the Rose playhouse, south of the Thames on the Bankside (now called the South Bank), not far from where the National Theatre now stands.

Henslowe kept detailed accounts of his affairs at the Rose, which still survive. They show that he controlled every aspect of the theatre, including choosing the players. He kept them on their toes, too – fining any who turned up late or drunk. He came to an arrangement with John Cholmley, a grocer, who paid Henslowe for the right to sell food and drink to the audience. They agreed to split the money taken at the performances between them, and Henslowe was always there to make sure he got his fair share.

Edward Alleyn, Phillip Henslowe's son-in-law and a leading actor in the company called the Admiral's Men.

EDWARD ALLEYN

Edward Alleyn came to the Rose as an actor in 1592 and he and his company, the Admiral's Men, settled there. Alleyn married Henslowe's stepdaughter, Joan. He played in at least two of Shakespeare's earliest plays but was best known for his performances of Christopher Marlowe's leading characters – Doctor Faustus and Tamburlaine. These parts demanded a highly dramatic, exaggerated style of acting which suited Alleyn.

COMPETITION BETWEEN COMPANIES

Costume was very important at the Rose, and Henslowe spent a large part of his profits on rich costumes and some spectacular pieces of scenery and special effects. When the Chamberlain's Men opened their new playhouse at the Globe in 1599, a stone's throw from the Rose, Henslowe decided it was time to open another theatre. He found a site north of the City, and here he had the Fortune built. Alleyn had retired from the stage by then but made a dramatic, and highly profitable, return.

Whilst the Chamberlain's Men were performing Shakespeare's more complicated comedies and great tragedies at the Globe, Henslowe offered a rougher, more popular entertainment. He put on plays by many different writers one of which, *The Roaring Girl*, dramatised the scandalous life of Marion Frith, a woman who took part in London low-life dressed as a man. She and her companions were often at the Fortune. She once shocked people by appearing briefly on stage:

'... in man's apparel and played upon her lute and sang a song.'

Alleyn's wife Joan, who was Henslowe's stepdaughter. She died in 1623, aged 52.

THE PURITAN BACKLASH

In the sixteenth century a form of Christianity called Puritanism developed. Its followers believed that people should have a direct relationship to God, expressed in a simple moral way of life which would 'purify' society. It was popular among the middle classes in Elizabethan England, and took root among Londoners. Although most Puritans were simply men and women trying to lead a good and honest life, there were extremists who were easily shocked and thought any sort of pleasure was wicked. It was men like these that Shakespeare made fun of in the character of Malvolio in *Twelfth Night*.

The Workes of William Shakespeare, containing all his Comedies, Histories, and Tragedies: Truely set forth, according to their first ORIGINALL.

The Names of the Principall Actors
in all these Playes.

William Shakespeare.
Richard Burbadge.
John Hemmings.
Augustine Phillips.
William Kempt.
Thomas Poope.
George Bryan.
Henry Condell.
William Slye.
Richard Cowly.
John Lowine.
Samuell Crosse.
Alexander Cooke.

Samuel Gilburne.
Robert Armin.
William Ostler.
Nathan Field.
John Underwood.
Nicholas Tooley.
William Ecclestone.
Joseph Taylor.
Robert Benfield.
Robert Goughe.
Richard Robinson.
John Shancke.
John Rice.

The title page of the First Folio, 1623, the first collected edition of Shakespeare's plays.

SOURCE OF WICKEDNESS

The players had always been the target of attacks by Puritan preachers, supported by important people in the City, which is why most of the theatres were in fact outside the City of London itself. Plays were thought to encourage bad behaviour; players to be dangerous men, who encouraged vice; and playhouses to be the source of wickedness and disease. The cramped conditions of theatre-going were seen as the breeding ground of the plague. When the disease was raging, the playhouses were among the first public buildings to be shut.

Preachers attacked plays and play-going ferociously, and the leaders of the City followed up the attacks with the weight of the law. But as long as the court and the nobility protected the players, and the playhouses remained popular, play-going continued.

TENSION BUILDS

Gradually however, public opinion shifted. It was not so much that plays became less popular as that a tension was building up which would lead to Civil War, the execution of King Charles I and the rise of Oliver Cromwell as Lord Protector. The Puritans were now a much more powerful force in the land. They thought that play-going was a part of the general wickedness of the nation which had to be swept away.

In 1633 William Prynne published a massive attack on the theatre. In his book, called *Histriomastix*, Prynne recalled how, as a young man, he had been to see four plays which contained:

'... such wickedness, such lewdness as then made my penitent heart to loath, my conscience to abhor all Stage-plays ever since.'

He continued with page after page, listing the supposed evil of the theatre, which didn't stop at implicating the court in its wickedness for allowing the Queen to perform in a masque. The book earned Prynne a £5000 fine, the loss of both his ears, and imprisonment in the Tower of London. But it was the sign of things to come. By 1642, the Puritans were in government and had issued a decree closing all public theatres. The Globe theatre was demolished two years later.

EUROPE

The plays were not forgotten, though. Companies travelled throughout Europe, where Shakespeare's plays continued to be popular. There were probably also some performances in private houses in England. When Charles II returned to England in 1660 it was not long before public theatres reopened. Shakespeare's plays were performed again, but were often seen as old fashioned. If they succeeded at all it was only after much rewriting. The first great age of English theatre was over.

INDEX